WORLD HISTORY Need to Know

SilverTip

World War II

by Daniel R. Faust

Consultant: Caitlin Krieck, Social Studies Teacher and Instructional Coach, The Lab School of Washington

BEARPORT
PUBLISHING

Minneapolis, Minnesota

Credits

Cover and title page, © Rob Crandall/Shutterstock; 5, © Imago History Collection/Alamy; 7, © UniversalImagesGroup/Getty Images; 9, © Roger Viollet/Getty Images; 11, © Mor65_Mauro Piccardi/Shutterstock; 13, © Lebrecht Music & Arts/Alamy; 17, © Victor Blackman/Getty Images; 18, © Russell Lee/Getty Images; 19, © Keystone/Getty Images; 21, © Bettmann/Getty Images; 23, © Fred Ramage/Getty Images; 25, © Bettmann/Getty Images; 27, © EQRoy/Shutterstock; 28, © Oasis World/Shutterstock.

Bearport Publishing Company Product Development Team

President: Jen Jenson; Director of Product Development: Spencer Brinker; Managing Editor: Allison Juda; Associate Editor: Naomi Reich; Associate Editor: Tiana Tran; Senior Designer: Colin O'Dea; Designer: Elena Klinkner; Designer: Kayla Eggert; Product Development Assistant: Owen Hamlin

A NOTE FROM THE PUBLISHER: Some of the historic photos in this book have been colorized to help readers have a more meaningful and rich experience. The color results are not intended to depict actual historical detail.

STATEMENT ON USAGE OF GENERATIVE ARTIFICIAL INTELLIGENCE
Bearport Publishing remains committed to publishing high-quality nonfiction books. Therefore, we restrict the use of generative AI to ensure accuracy of all text and visual components pertaining to a book's subject. See BearportPublishing.com for details.

Library of Congress Cataloging-in-Publication Data

Names: Faust, Daniel R., author.
Title: World War II / by Daniel R. Faust.
Other titles: World War Two
Description: Minneapolis, Minnesota : Bearport Publishing Company, [2024] |
  Series: World history: need to know | Includes bibliographical
  references and index.
Identifiers: LCCN 2023035714 (print) | LCCN 2023035715 (ebook) | ISBN
  9798889165477 (library binding) | ISBN 9798889165545 (paperback) | ISBN
  9798889165606 (ebook)
Subjects: LCSH: World War, 1939-1945–Juvenile literature.
Classification: LCC D743.7 .F38 2024 (print) | LCC D743.7 (ebook) | DDC
  940.54–dc23/eng/20230803
LC record available at https://lccn.loc.gov/2023035714
LC ebook record available at https://lccn.loc.gov/2023035715

Copyright © 2024 Bearport Publishing Company. All rights reserved. No part of this publication may be reproduced in whole or in part, stored in any retrieval system, or transmitted in any form or by any means, electronic, mechanical, photocopying, recording, or otherwise, without written permission from the publisher.

For more information, write to Bearport Publishing, 5357 Penn Avenue South, Minneapolis, MN 55419.

Contents

Invasion........................ 4
Germany Hurting................. 6
The Holocaust................... 10
The Rise of Dictators........... 12
War Begins...................... 14
Turning Points.................. 18
The War Ends.................... 22
Steps toward Peace.............. 26

The World at War................28
SilverTips for Success..........29
Glossary........................30
Read More.......................31
Learn More Online...............31
Index...........................32
About the Author................32

Invasion

On September 1, 1939, the German army **invaded** Poland. Days later, Britain and France **declared** war on Germany. World War II had begun.

What led to this moment? It all started with another global war two decades earlier.

From 1914 until 1918, Europe was torn apart. Britain, France, Russia, Germany, and Austria-Hungary were battling World War I. At first, this fighting was called the Great War. Nobody thought anything like it would happen again.

Germany Hurting

By the end of World War I, Germany was struggling. The country's **economy** was weak after the expensive war. Then, Germany was blamed for the fighting. Germany was forced to give up land. It had to pay for causing the war. The punishments made things even worse for the country.

Germany's economy was not the only one struggling. Other countries where the war was fought also faced hard times. Eventually, the problem spread. This period became known as the Great Depression.

During this time, it took stacks of money to buy small things in Germany.

Many Germans lost their jobs. Some could not pay for basic needs, such as food and clothes. The people were scared and angry.

They turned to a new leader. Adolf Hitler rose to power. He promised to help Germany. He falsely blamed the country's problems on Jewish people.

> Hitler was the leader of the Nazi Party. The Nazis believed Germany was the greatest country in the world. They said their people were the best. All others were beneath them.

The Holocaust

Many people in Germany turned against Jews. Over the years that followed, Jewish people in Nazi-controlled areas lost their rights. They were sent to **concentration camps** where many were killed. About 6 million Jews died in these camps by the end of World War II. This became known as the Holocaust.

The Nazis also targeted other groups. They attacked gay people, people with disabilities, and members of the Roma community. People from these groups were sent to concentration camps along with Jews.

Auschwitz concentration camp

More than 1 million people were killed at Auschwitz concentration camp.

The Rise of Dictators

The Nazi party took control of Germany in 1933. Hitler became **dictator**. He had total power over Germany, but he wanted more. And there were other leaders like him around the world.

In 1937, Japan invaded China. A year later, Hitler took Austria.

> Hitler was not the only dictator of his time. Benito Mussolini had been dictator of Italy since the 1920s. Francisco Franco became the dictator of Spain in 1939.

War Begins

At first, other countries let Hitler do what he wanted. They did not want another war. This changed when Germany invaded Poland.

Britain and France were the first to stand against Germany. They were joined by Australia, New Zealand, South Africa, and Canada. Italy and Japan sided with Germany.

> Italy, Japan, and Germany were called the Axis powers. The countries against them were known as the Allies. The Soviet Union supported Germany at first. It switched to the Allies later.

Early Countries in World War II

The war picked up quickly. Between May and June 1940, Germany took over much of western Europe. The Nazis gained ground in Belgium and northern France.

From July until October, the German air force bombed major cities in Britain. This was called the Battle of Britain.

World War II became a true global war. Fighting raged across Europe, Asia, and Africa. Airplanes bombed enemies from the sky. Navies fought at sea.

The Battle of Britain

Turning Points

On December 7, 1941, Japanese planes bombed the U.S. Navy base at Pearl Harbor. Before then, the United States had not been a part of the war. But they could not ignore this attack. The United States joined the Allies.

Not long after Pearl Harbor, Japan took control over much of Southeast Asia. This included islands in the Pacific Ocean. The U.S. and Japanese navies fought many battles in the Pacific.

Pearl Harbor on Oahu Island, Hawaii

Over the next few years, the Axis powers took over most of Europe. The Allies had to do something big. On June 6, 1944, they attacked the German army in Normandy, France. The Allies won this battle along the northern coast. They began moving east toward Germany.

About 150,000 Allied soldiers crossed the English Channel to get to Normandy. They arrived early in the morning. Then, the Allied forces rushed at the German troops in a surprise attack.

The attack at Normandy is sometimes called D-Day.

The War Ends

Germany was trapped. The Soviet Union was closing in from the east. Britain, France, and the U.S. were coming from the west. Germany tried to put up one last fight at the Battle of the Bulge. However, they failed. The Allies won. They took over Germany. Germany **surrendered** in May 1945.

> The Battle of the Bulge lasted for about a month. By the end of the fighting, 120,000 German soldiers had died. The Allied forces lost 75,000 people.

Still, fighting continued in the Pacific. The United States had pushed the Japanese army back to Japan. But Japan would not give in.

Then, the United States tried a new weapon. They dropped **atomic bombs** on Japan. Japan surrendered on September 2, 1945.

> The United States dropped two atomic bombs. The first landed on the city of Hiroshima. The second hit Nagasaki. Both cities were destroyed. More than 100,000 people were killed.

The destruction from the bomb in Nagasaki

Steps toward Peace

Within thirty years, there had been two global wars. Countries around the world did not want to fight another one. So, the Allied forces formed the United Nations. Here, countries would meet to talk about their problems. They would work together. People hoped this would prevent any future world wars.

> We don't know for sure how many people died during World War II. It was hard to keep good records during the fighting. However, most experts think between 35 and 60 million people died.

The World at War

World War II was fought between two sides. The Allied forces and the Axis powers had support from countries around the world. Who were their key members?

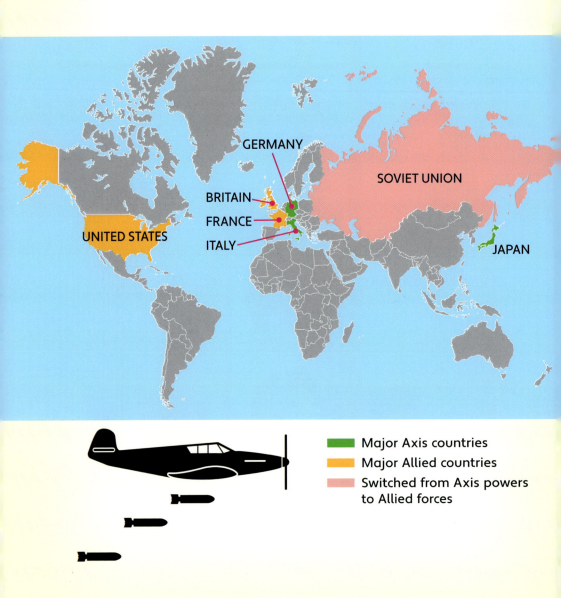

Major Axis countries
Major Allied countries
Switched from Axis powers to Allied forces

SilverTips for SUCCESS

★ SilverTips for REVIEW

Review what you've learned. Use the text to help you.

Define key terms

Allied forces
Axis powers
Battle at Normandy
Hitler, Adolf
Holocaust

Check for understanding

What were some of the major causes of World War II?

Name the two sides who fought in World War II and which countries belonged to each.

What event led to the United States joining World War II?

Think deeper

How might your life today be different if the second world war ended differently?

★ SilverTips on TEST-TAKING

- **Make a study plan.** Ask your teacher what the test is going to cover. Then, set aside time to study a little bit every day.

- **Read all the questions carefully.** Be sure you know what is being asked.

- **Skip any questions** you don't know how to answer right away. Mark them and come back later if you have time.

Glossary

atomic bombs very powerful bombs that can destroy entire cities

concentration camps places where prisoners of war are held and often killed

declared stated strongly and officially

dictator a person who has complete control over a country

economy the system of buying, selling, making things, and managing money in a place

invaded entered by force or took over, usually in a harmful way

surrendered agreed to give up fighting

Read More

Breach, Jen. *Daring Women of D-Day: Bold Spies of World War II (Women Warriors of World War II).* North Mankato, MN: Capstone Press, 2024.

Lake, Theia. *The Tuskegee Airmen (Great Figures in Black History).* Buffalo, NY: PowerKids Press, 2024.

Monroe, Alex. *World War II (Torque: War Histories).* Minneapolis: Bellwether Media, 2024.

Learn More Online

1. Go to **www.factsurfer.com** or scan the QR code below.

2. Enter "**World War II**" into the search box.

3. Click on the cover of this book to see a list of websites.

Index

Allied forces 14–15, 18, 20, 22, 26, 28

atomic bomb 24–25

Axis powers 14–15, 20, 28

Britain 4, 14–17, 20, 22, 28

concentration camps 10–11

France 4, 14–16, 20, 22, 28

Germany 4, 6–8, 10, 12, 14–16, 20, 22, 28

Hitler, Adolf 8–9, 12, 14

Italy 12, 14–15, 28

Japan 12, 14–15, 18, 24, 28

Jews 8, 10

Nazi Party 8, 10, 12, 16

Soviet Union 14–15, 22, 28

United Nations, the 26–27

United States 18, 22, 24, 28

About the Author

Daniel R. Faust is a freelance writer of fiction and nonfiction. He lives in Queens, NY.